How To Get Rid Of Guilt

Practical Steps on How to Stop Feeling Guilty

John Annabel

Table of Contents

Chapter 1

Understanding the Sources of Guilt

According to the American Psychological Association (APA), guilt is a self-conscious emotion characterized by a painful appraisal of having done or thought something wrong, and often by a willingness to take action to undo or mitigate this wrong. While some guilt can be beneficial and help us make better decisions, excessive or uncontrollable guilt can be harmful to our physical and mental health. If you are frequently plagued by guilt or are overwhelmed by a deep sense of guilt, understanding where the feeling comes from and learning to manage it can help you move forward in a healthy manner.

An "appropriate" sense of guilt is one that serves a useful purpose before dissipating. For example, feeling guilty for wronging someone can help motivate you to apologize and/or make things right. It may also assist you in avoiding similar harmful behavior in the future. A guilt complex, also known as "irrational guilt," is when you feel a persistent sense of guilt over time that isn't always tied to a specific wrong. It could also appear as a constant, tense fear of doing something wrong. Individuals who tend to feel this way are described as "guilt-prone," with those who were socialized and/or identify as women being more guilt-prone.

It's also worth noting that excessive guilt, as well as a complete lack of guilt or remorse, may be associated with certain mental health issues. Excessive guilt, for example, could fuel compulsions in someone suffering from obsessive-compulsive disorder (OCD). Feelings of guilt may also contribute to depression symptoms, as constantly believing that you're doing things wrong or not doing enough can have a negative impact on one's self-worth, life outlook, and overall mental health. Anxiety disorders may be caused by or contribute to a guilt complex. A lack of guilt, on the other hand, may be indicative of a personality disorder, such as antisocial personality disorder.

Guilt Factors

If you're experiencing feelings of guilt, understanding the underlying cause can help you work toward resolution.

When it comes to appropriate guilt, the cause is usually action or inaction that violates an individual's moral code or the moral code of the larger culture or society in which they live. This type of guilt can develop naturally within a person or be imposed on them by others. Someone who gossips or speaks negatively about a friend behind their friend's back, for example, may feel guilty after doing so or after being reprimanded by someone else in their social circle.

The causes of a guilt complex vary, but they frequently involve a distorted sense of responsibility or unrealistically high standards imposed on someone during childhood or in a relationship. Some people, for example, who grew up in strict religious traditions that left little room for error and promised terrifying punishments for wrongdoing may develop a guilt complex. Those who were raised by perfectionist parents or caregivers, or who were in a relationship with such a person as an adult, may also experience a guilt complex as a result of their human inability to behave perfectly all of the time. Someone who has experienced childhood trauma or a difficult upbringing may feel guilty about the events, even if they were not responsible for them. Similarly, surviving a fatal event while others did not may result in the experience and pain of survivor's guilt.

Chapter 2

Recognizing Unhealthy Guilt

"Why do I feel so guilty about such minor things?" Guilt is an emotion that everyone feels at some point in their lives. It has the potential to be a healthy emotion that helps us learn from our mistakes and become better versions of ourselves. It can also serve as a reminder of our moral compass, prompting us to reflect on our actions and make amends. When guilt becomes excessive, all-consuming, and irrational, it can develop into a crippling condition known as unhealthy guilt syndrome.

Unhealthy Guilt Syndrome (UGS), also known as pathological guilt, is a psychological condition in which a person feels excessive and irrational guilt for past actions or events. If you've ever wondered, "Why do I feel so guilty over small things?", it could be due to UGS. It describes the sensation of excessive, chronic guilt that interferes with normal functioning. It stems from a distorted understanding of responsibility and blame. People who suffer from unhealthy guilt tend to hold themselves to unreasonable standards and blame themselves for things over which they have no control.

This guilt is frequently exaggerated in relation to the situation and can persist even when the individual has done nothing wrong. People who suffer from unhealthy guilt frequently believe that they are to blame for the actions and feelings of others, even when they are not. They may constantly apologize for things that are not their fault and feel guilty for things over which they have no control. Now that we've defined unhealthy guilt syndrome, let's look at the distinction between healthy and unhealthy guilt.

Healthy vs. Unhealthy Guilt

Guilt is a normal human emotion that we all experience on occasion. It is a healthy emotion that allows us to learn from our mistakes and make amends. Guilt, on the other hand, can become excessive and irrational, leading to unhealthy or pathological guilt. Understanding the definition of unhealthy guilt syndrome can help us realize that the main difference between healthy and unhealthy guilt is the extent and duration of the guilt.

Healthy guilt is a fleeting emotion that arises when we act in a way that contradicts our values or beliefs. It is a signal that we must accept responsibility for our actions and, if necessary, make amends. Once we've done that, the guilt fades and we can move on. Unhealthy guilt, on the other hand, is a persistent feeling of guilt that persists long after we have accepted responsibility for our actions. It is frequently out of proportion to the situation and can be triggered by events beyond our control. Unhealthy guilt can be crippling, causing feelings of worthlessness, self-blame, and depression. Healthy guilt is a fleeting emotion that acts as a guidepost for our actions.

Unhealthy guilt is a pervasive sense of guilt that can be crippling and irrational. It is critical to distinguish between the two and take steps to address unhealthy guilt if it arises.

Symptoms Of An Unhealthy Guilt Complex

UGS symptoms differ from person to person. The following are some of the most common emotional and physical signs of guilt:

Excessive remorse People who suffer from unhealthy guilt frequently feel guilty about things that are not their fault and may apologize excessively.

Self-blame Blaming yourself is one of the symptoms of guilt. They may constantly blame themselves for previous events or actions, even if they are not at fault.

Self-esteem issues Low self-esteem and feelings of worthlessness can also result from pathological guilt. This is one of the most telling signs that someone is feeling guilty because they are constantly apologizing.

Anxiety Anxiety is a common manifestation of unhealthy guilt syndrome. People may be overly concerned with the consequences of their actions or fear being judged by others.

Depression UGS can also cause depression, which is characterized by sadness, hopelessness, and a loss of interest in activities. This is one of the most common signs that someone is feeling guilty.

Unhealthy guilt can also manifest as physical symptoms of guilt, *such as*:

- ★ *Tiredness*
- ★ *Sleeplessness*
- ★ *Muscle tenseness*
- ★ *Headaches*
- ★ *Digestive problems like nausea, vomiting, stomach pain, and diarrhea.*

Other physical symptoms of guilt may exist in addition to these. It is important to note that these physical symptoms of guilt can be caused by a variety of other factors. Now that we've covered the physical manifestations of guilt, let's look at some of the emotional manifestations of guilt.

Other commonly observed symptoms of unhealthy *guilt include*:

- ★ *Excessive apology*
- ★ *Difficulties making decisions due to apprehension about making mistakes*
- ★ *Persistent feelings of worthlessness, inadequacy, and self-hatred*
- ★ *Constant ruminating or dwelling on perceived flaws and failures*
- ★ *Feelings of guilt that are out of proportion to the situation or offense*
- ★ *Feeling guilty about trivial or insignificant issues*

★ *Difficulties feeling joy or pleasure*
★ *Isolation and social withdrawal*

Identifying the physical and emotional signs of guilt can assist us in better managing our unhealthy guilt.

The Source Of The Unhealthy Guilt Syndrome

Pathological guilt can be caused by a variety of underlying factors and causes, *including*:

Childhood memories
Childhood traumas such as abuse, neglect, or excessive criticism can result in the development of unhealthy guilt. Children who are constantly blamed for things that are not their fault may grow up feeling responsible for everything.

Trauma
Past trauma, particularly from childhood, can lead to unhealthy guilt about not being able to prevent or avoid the trauma. UGS can also be triggered by traumatic events such as car accidents, natural disasters, or violence. Trauma survivors may feel guilty for surviving while others did not or for not being able to prevent the traumatic event from occurring. This is why you wonder, "Why do I feel so guilty over such trivial matters?"

Mental health issues
Unhealthy guilt syndrome is frequently linked to mental health issues such as depression, anxiety, or obsessive-compulsive disorder (OCD). These conditions can cause people to overthink past events and feel guilty about things over which they have no control.

Personality characteristics
People with certain personality traits, such as perfectionism or high sensitivity, may be predisposed to pathological guilt. They may have

high expectations of themselves and feel guilty when they fail to meet them. Other possible underlying factors include:

The chemistry of the brain
Chemical imbalances in the brain can lower a person's ability to feel guilty.

Strict upbringing

Individuals raised by authoritarian parents with rigid, "black-and-white" rules are prone to harsh self-judgment and guilt. To please others at all costs frequently leads to imposing unrealistic demands and feeling guilty when they are not met. This is another reason you may be wondering, "Why do I feel so guilty over such insignificant things?"

Unhealthy Guilt Syndrome And Guilt Complex

The guilt complex and the unhealthy guilt syndrome are not the same thing. Guilt complex is a chronic pattern of excessive guilt, whereas UGS is a more acute, irrational, and intense form of guilt that is triggered by specific events or situations.

A guilt complex is a psychological condition in which a person feels excessive guilt and self-blame for their actions or thoughts. It is frequently a long-term pattern resulting from childhood experiences or trauma. UGS, on the other hand, is a condition in which a person feels excessive and irrational guilt for past actions or events. This guilt is frequently exaggerated in relation to the situation and can persist even when the individual has done nothing wrong.

While the causes and symptoms of guilt complex are similar to those of unhealthy guilt syndrome, they are distinct psychological phenomena.

There is a distinction between guilt complex and unhealthy guilt syndrome.

Now that we know the meanings of UGS and guilt complex are not the same, here are some key differences between guilt complex and pathological guilt syndrome:

Nature
The guilt complex is a long-term pattern of excessive guilt and self-blame, whereas unhealthy guilt is a more acute and intense form of guilt triggered by specific events or situations.

Duration
The guilt complex is a persistent pattern of excessive guilt that can last for years or even a lifetime, whereas UGS can come and go but is more acute and lasts for a shorter period of time.

Causes
Guilt complexes are frequently caused by childhood experiences or trauma, whereas pathological guilt can be caused by a variety of factors such as mental health conditions, personality traits, or specific events.

Symptoms
Low self-esteem, self-blame, and anxiety are all symptoms of unhealthy guilt and guilt complex, but UGS can also cause excessive apologizing, feeling responsible for others' feelings, and a persistent sense of guilt. While the symptoms of guilt complex may be similar, the experiences may differ.

Treatment
Treatment for guilt complex may include therapy to assist individuals in processing past experiences and developing coping strategies, whereas treatment for unhealthy guilt syndrome may include therapy, medication, or a combination of the two, depending on the underlying causes. Guilt complex causes can be treated with cognitive-behavioral therapy (CBT), which focuses on changing negative thought patterns and behaviors, whereas UGS can be treated with exposure therapy, which involves gradually exposing

people to triggering situations or thoughts in order to reduce anxiety and guilt.

Relationship with other mental illnesses
Guilt complex is frequently associated with depression, anxiety, and post-traumatic stress disorder (PTSD), whereas unhealthy guilt is frequently associated with obsessive-compulsive disorder (OCD), generalized anxiety disorder (GAD), or borderline personality disorder (BPD).

Influence On Daily Life

The guilt complex and UGS can both have an impact on a person's day-to-day life, relationships, and overall well-being. Avoiding guilt complex treatment can result in isolation, self-doubt, and a sense of hopelessness, whereas unhealthy guilt can cause people to avoid social interactions, ruminate excessively on past events, and experience physical symptoms like headaches or stomach aches.

Prognosis
The prognosis for guilt complex and unhealthy guilt syndrome varies according to the individual's situation. The severity of the underlying trauma or experiences, as well as the individual's willingness to engage in therapy, may influence the prognosis for guilt-complex treatment. The prognosis for UGS may be affected by the underlying causes as well as the effectiveness of the treatment approach. Individuals with both guilt complex and unhealthy guilt, with proper treatment and support, can learn to manage their symptoms and improve their overall quality of life.

Unhealthy guilt can have serious consequences for a person's emotional, psychological, and physical well-being. Here are some examples of how guilt can affect a person:

Self-esteem issues
People suffering from UGS may believe they are to blame for everything that goes wrong in their lives and may feel guilty about their perceived shortcomings.

Anxiety
People who suffer from unhealthy guilt may be overly concerned about the consequences of their actions or fear being judged by others.

Depression
Unhealthy guilt can also lead to depression, leaving a person feeling sad, hopeless, or like a burden to others. This is one of the most damaging effects of guilt on a person.

Physical Manifestations Of Guilt

Unhealthy guilt can also have an effect on a person's physical health, causing symptoms such as headaches, stomachaches, and fatigue.

Relationship difficulties
It can have an impact on your relationships. Unhealthy guilt can sever bonds with family, friends, and romantic partners. People who suffer from excessive guilt may constantly apologize or avoid social situations.

Decision-making impairment
Unhealthy guilt can also impair a person's decision-making ability. For fear of making a mistake, they may be hesitant to take risks or make decisions.

Healing from unhealthy guilt syndrome entails changing one's perspective, and adopting a more balanced, self-compassionate view of oneself and one's role and responsibilities in the world. While it is not easy, people who are truly burdened by unhealthy guilt can find relief through the strategies outlined above, regaining control over this crippling syndrome. Even those who have struggled with guilt their entire lives can come to experience life in a new, guilt-free way with courage, patience, and a willingness to change.

Chapter 3

The Effects of Shame and Guilt on Mental Health

Two of the most agonizing human emotions are guilt and shame. Who wants constant reminders that we cheated on a friend, failed an exam, or let a family member down? However, while guilt and shame are unpleasant emotions, they are not harmful.

While guilt and shame can cause depression, anxiety, and paranoia, they can also prompt us to act more responsibly. When we do something we are not proud of, the brain sends out a signal that prompts us to change our behavior. Guilt and shame play an important adaptive function in human survival. The origins of this pair of emotions, as well as how they function in the brain.

Shame has long been considered the toxic cousin of guilt, but it has aided our evolution. Shame and guilt are functionally designed to keep us from harming those we care about and to motivate us to behave better in the future. People in foraging societies had to rely on one another to survive disease, predators, and scarcity of resources. Being disliked could result in death because no one will look out for you or share with you.

Guilt can make us more compassionate and generous. Imposing costs on those who care about your well-being, such as family and friends, has an indirect cost for the individual. The guilt system is intended to detect the imposition of this harm, stop it, and correct it. Similarly, shame alerts us when we act in ways that may cause others to devalue us and refuse to help us. As a result, natural selection favors those who experience guilt and shame.

The Distinction Between Guilt And Shame

Guilt and shame are self-conscious feelings associated with actual or perceived moral failings. Their motivations and outcomes, however, are distinct, and you can have one without the other.

Guilt can occur even if no one else is aware of what you did. There may be no repercussions other than the feeling that you should treat the other person better in the future. You may also attempt to right the wrong.

The emphasis of shame is on someone else discovering your wrongdoing. In contrast to guilt, shame can lead to additional transgressions such as lying or destroying evidence. These are transgressions in the sense that they are socially unacceptable, particularly for the victims. However, these behaviors may reduce the likelihood that the offender is devalued by others, which is the function of shame.

The operation of the brain
Guilt and shame have some neural networks in the frontal and temporal areas of the brain in common, but their patterns are very different. Guilt arises when your actions contradict your conscience. When we believe we have harmed our reputation, we experience shame.

During fMRI studies, shame activated the right side of the brain but not the amygdala. There was activity in the amygdala and frontal lobes during the guilt state, but less neural activity in both brain hemispheres. The researchers came to the conclusion that shame, with its broad cultural and social factors, is a more complex emotion than guilt, which is only linked to a person's learned social standards.

Individuals' Guilt and Shame

Biology and environment both influence behavior, so many factors come into play. The shame system accurately predicts and precisely matches the degree to which others will devalue you if you engage in a particular action that they disapprove of. In this way, the shame system embodies the Goldilocks principle: it activates to the "just right" degree. In the case of guilt, the intensity is related to the individual's internal value system rather than that of others.

Some psychiatric conditions, such as psychopathy, may cause people to feel no shame or guilt. Children who are raised to feel a lot of guilt and shame are more likely to carry on that pattern as adults.

What to Do When You're Overwhelmed by Guilt

Taking the time to consider where your guilt came from and whether it is appropriate or irrational can help you decide what to do next. If your action or inaction caused someone harm that a reasonable person would agree was your fault, you may take steps to correct the situation. This could include apologizing and making amends in other ways.

If you are experiencing "irrational" guilt as part of a guilt complex and/or mental health condition, there are a few strategies you can try to manage it so that it does not interfere with your life or cause further distress. Among these are the following:

Determine the source
If you notice that a certain person is constantly encouraging you to feel guilty when you shouldn't, you should consider spending less time with them and seeing if your feelings improve. The same can be said for social media; unfollowing accounts that make you feel guilty or deleting your account entirely if it's contributing to irrational guilt feelings could be beneficial. If you can trace your guilt complex back

to a traumatic event or a difficult upbringing, journaling and/or therapy may be helpful.

Consider someone you care about in your situation
Consider what you would say to a friend or family member who came to you to confess that they were feeling guilty for the same reason you are now. You might try to apply that perspective to yourself if you comfort them and assure them that it's not their fault or that it's not reasonable to feel guilty for this particular situation. This is a self-compassion exercise, which according to research can help improve well-being by making you feel cared for, connected, and emotionally calm.

Keep a Journal About It
Sometimes the stories we tell ourselves in our heads can make us feel bad until they are exposed. In other words, journaling or speaking aloud about the situation that causes you irrational guilt may help you see it for what it is and let go of the guilt you feel. Putting your feelings and thoughts into words and contextualizing the situation verbally or in writing can help you see the truth.

Consult a Therapist
Speaking with a therapist is another potentially beneficial method of dealing with guilt, regardless of its source. A therapist can help you cope if you are experiencing appropriate guilt for an action you took that you cannot change. A therapist can provide you with a safe space to express your emotions, learn healthy coping techniques, and address any other symptoms if you have a guilt complex and/or experience it as a result of a mental health issue. In any case, having access to their nonjudgmental, unbiased listening and support can be beneficial for anyone who is experiencing feelings of guilt for any reason.

Chapter 4

Self-Forgiveness

We often hear how important it is to forgive those who have wronged us, but what about forgiving ourselves? Is that also important? Absolutely. When we hurt others, we feel regret and apologize, hoping to make things right. However, we frequently punish ourselves for mistakes and develop negative self-images as a result. These experiences are accompanied by feelings of shame and guilt; while these feelings are similar and can occur concurrently, they are slightly different.

Guilt and Shame

Shame and guilt can feel very similar, as discussed in the previous chapter; in both cases, we feel bad about ourselves. However, guilt can be defined as a sense of disappointment in oneself for violating an important internal value or code of behavior. Feeling guilty can be beneficial because it can lead to positive behavior change. With shame, one may also experience self-dissatisfaction, but no value has been violated. We feel guilty when we feel bad about something we did or did not do. When we are ashamed, we feel bad about ourselves. When we feel guilty, we must learn that it is acceptable to make mistakes. When we feel ashamed, we must learn that it is okay to be ourselves.

Shame is harmful because it causes feelings of unworthiness and reinforces a negative self-image. Shame, among other emotions, can cause self-criticism, self-blame, self-neglect, self-destructive behavior, self-sabotaging behavior, the belief that you do not deserve good things and anger.

Self-Forgiveness

Self-forgiveness, especially in the face of shame. Self-forgiveness promotes emotional stability and mental peace. The more shame you heal, the more clearly you will be able to see yourself, flaws and all. You will be able to recognize and admit to yourself and others how you have harmed them. Shame can be overcome through compassion. Self-compassion works to neutralize shame and remove the toxins that shame creates. Self-forgiveness is an essential component of self-compassion. It relieves the pain caused by shame in our body, mind, and soul, and it aids in the overall healing process.

Self-Understanding

Understanding the experiences, traumas, and stressors that have led to the development of negative thought patterns in your life can help you forgive yourself for the ways you have hurt yourself or others. Understanding the reasoning behind your coping mechanisms or beliefs can help you stop blaming yourself for decisions you may or may not have made.

According to research, the long-term effects of trauma are most visible and noticeable when people are stressed, in new situations, or in situations that remind them of the circumstances of their trauma. As a result, situations can sometimes elicit reactions that we wish we hadn't. Understanding yourself through healthy coping skills, therapy, and support, on the other hand, can significantly improve your ability to forgive and move forward.

Developing Self-Compassion

We've all made mistakes. Knowing this and realizing you are not alone can help you have compassion for and forgive yourself. Compassion for yourself does not absolve you of responsibility for your actions, but it can free you from negative self-talk that keeps you from forgiving yourself and allows you to respond to the situation with clarity.

When you examine your mistakes, it becomes clear that you did not consciously choose to make them, and even when you did, the motivation for your actions was influenced by other experiences. Specific patterns formed as a result of the shame you carried, outside circumstances, and additional stressors. These external factors can include genetics, family experiences, and life circumstances.

When we recognize that we are the result of numerous factors, we can stop taking our 'personal failings' so personally. We can be less judgmental of ourselves and others when we recognize the intricate web of causes and conditions in which we are all entangled. A deep understanding of interconnectedness allows us to have compassion for the fact that we're doing our best with the cards life has dealt us.

Obtaining Pardon

If you are having difficulty engaging in self-forgiveness, be open and curious with yourself. "Why wouldn't I want to forgive myself?" ask yourself. If you say, "I don't deserve it," you're expressing your shame. If you still think you don't deserve forgiveness, you might think you have to earn it.

Be truthful about what you believe you need forgiveness for. Be honest with yourself about what you believe you have done, as this may help you shift some negative beliefs and become more compassionate and forgiving toward yourself.

Chapter 5

Apologizing and Making Restitution

One of the most difficult things you'll ever have to do is apologize. An apology is frequently the result of some wrongdoing, where feelings are hurt and mistakes accumulate. We've all found ourselves in situations where we needed to apologize. Perhaps you said something hurtful unintentionally or failed to keep a promise. Perhaps things went wrong as a result of your inaction. Apologies, for whatever reason, should be a part of our lives because no one is perfect. Many people, however, struggle with it because they don't know how to apologize.

Part of this stems from the difficulty of admitting we need to apologize in the first place. Our pride frequently gets the best of us. We don't want to admit we messed up or crossed the line. At times, immaturity rears its ugly head, making us the most obstinate when we need to accept our flaws. According to one study, other barriers include having little to no empathy for the victim. However, once you've learned how to apologize to someone, you'll come to regard it as a skill, and the more practice you put in, the easier it will become. You'll be able to make amends instead of making excuses.

The Essential Elements of a Sincere Apology

Apologies are not intended to change the past; rather, they are intended to change the future. While writing a genuine and effective apology may appear to be an art form, there is some science to it. Researchers from Ohio State University's Fisher College of Business discovered that the best apologies had six components. These components are as follows:

Regret expression

When you express regret, you demonstrate to the offended party that you are sorry for what you did or, in some cases, did not do. You deeply regret how you made them feel, and you want nothing more than to make things right. By displaying remorse in this manner, you demonstrate how important it is to you that you make a correction.

Description of what went wrong

By describing what happened in detail, you demonstrate that you have a thorough understanding of the situation. It rules out the possibility that the conflict was caused solely by a difference of opinion.

Acceptance of responsibility

It ensures that you are not saying meaningless things. Instead, you acknowledge the role you played in requiring an apology in the first place. This is your chance to accept responsibility for what you did. By accepting responsibility, you demonstrate that you are not passing the buck to someone else or to unforeseeable circumstances. This is your mess, and you're attempting to clean it.

Repentance declaration

A declaration of repentance is a promise to yourself that you will change your behavior in the future. Not only are you promising not to make the same mistake again, but you are also promising not to cause more problems with the same actions or behaviors.

Repair suggestion

Saying you'll change isn't enough. You must also repair the damage you have caused. This could be physical damage, or it could be emotional or mental damage. It is important to note that some parties may reject your offer, which is perfectly fine. The important thing is to make an offer so they can make a decision.

Beseech forgiveness

The final step is to ask for forgiveness from the injured party. Again, it is their choice, but making that request demonstrates your sincerity in making amends.

Some of these components, according to one of the study's authors, are more important than others. According to our findings, the most important component is an acceptance of responsibility. Say you made a mistake and it's your fault. Second came the offer to repair the damage. One issue with apologies is that words are cheap. However, by saying, 'I'll fix what's wrong,' you commit to taking action to repair the damage.

Although researchers discovered six essential components for heartfelt apologies, other elements can be effective additions.

★ *While a late apology is preferable to none, the closer you apologize to the offending incident, the better.*

★ *Make it clear that you're apologizing because you made a mistake, not because you want someone to stop bothering you.*

★ *Create a positive vision of what will happen after you have done everything possible to correct your errors.*

Commitment: This is a willingness to go to any length to make things right.
Reasons to Apologize to Someone You've Offended
Saying sorry to someone is difficult, but putting your pride aside for someone is the most difficult. Nobody is perfect, which is why understanding how to apologize to someone is critical. You don't want to permanently sever a relationship, whether in your personal or professional life. You also don't want your mistakes to go uncorrected.

A sincere apology can help to repair the damage and mend fences. Learning how to say sorry benefits both you and the person receiving the apology. Here are just a few of the advantages of apologizing:

★ *Improved emotional healing as a result*
★ *Allows the giver to no longer regard the wrongdoer as someone to fear.*

25

- ★ *Opportunities for empathy and forgiveness are created.*
- ★ *Enhances a person's humility*
- ★ *This prevents people from making similar mistakes in the future*
- ★ *Improves self-esteem*
- ★ *Assists people in moving on*
- ★ *Increases the depth of connections and relationships*

It's difficult enough to apologize. Making it even more difficult is doing so face-to-face. Face-to-face apologies require a great deal of courage and bravery, not to mention how vulnerable they can make you feel. Regardless of the unpleasant feelings that may arise during an apology, it is best to select this option when it is available. However, there are some circumstances in which writing may be preferable. Here are a few examples:

You may not be able to apologize to the person in person. This is frequently the case when the offense is particularly serious.

When you need to be absolutely certain that the wording is perfect. Writing allows you to go back over your words and make sure they come across the way you want them to. When you have social anxiety or find it difficult to interact with others.

If you choose to write your apology, follow the same guidelines as discussed above. *Consider the following*:

Avoid using passive language that gives the impression of avoiding responsibility. You also don't want your apology to sound like a corporate public relations statement.

Certain words are used to improve an apology. Certain intensifiers like, 'very,' 'truly,' 'sincerely,' 'extremely,' or 'awfully' in front of the word'sorry' or words like 'utmost' or 'heartfelt' in front of the word 'apology' can strengthen it.

Common Apology Problems

One of the most overlooked conflict resolution skills is the ability to apologize. And, as with any skill, mistakes are common. *Here are some of the most common apologetic errors:*

- ★ *Using ambiguous language*
- ★ *Making excuses or avoiding responsibility*
- ★ *Rambling or frequently changing the subject*
- ★ *Obligatory apologies rather than genuine concern*
- ★ *Failure to hold yourself responsible*
- ★ *Putting pressure on the victim for immediate forgiveness*
- ★ *Postponing an apology*
- ★ *Inability to empathize with the victim*
- ★ *Not following through on your apology or promise*
- ★ *Allowing the offense to occur repeatedly*

Many of these errors can be avoided by being direct and admitting what you did. Apologies should be made from the heart after you have gained a true understanding of the pain your actions have caused. Accept responsibility for the problem and do everything possible to correct it.

At the same time, you must recognize that forgiveness takes time, particularly for serious offenses. People require space and time to recover. Even if they forgive you, it may take some time for them to fully trust you. People will come around if you demonstrate a commitment to making things right.

Chapter 6

Developing a Positive Attitude

Every morning, we are reborn. The most important thing is what we do today, I recall how I used to think; it was always, People stink and I despise.... Because I was constantly focusing on the negative aspects of humanity, that was all I could see. It casts a shadow that sapped the joy from life. It should have been obvious that I was causing my own misery, but I couldn't see how my own thoughts were influencing my mood.

I had to change my entire perspective by training my mind to see things in a different light. It would have been simple to continue on the same path. After all, I had chronic fatigue, no money, and nothing to look forward to because I lacked a compelling future vision. I believed the current situation was permanent.

I finally had enough and began to consider what I could do to improve my situation. As I worked on my mindset, a new path that was previously unknown to me began to emerge. My goals and dreams grew larger and more ambitious as time passed. I began to fantasize about being fit and healthy, running my own business, and traveling the world. These are some of the steps I took to improve my mindset and my life.

Seek out positive people
A negative social circle serves as an echo chamber for negative ideas. A positive social circle will act as an echo chamber, but one that will help you achieve your goals, so choose your friends wisely.

Look for people who share the values you want to live by. Join online groups and attend networking or social events centered on personal development. As your own mind begins to change, it will become easier to connect with more positive people. I'm not suggesting you abandon friends who are going through a difficult time and need your support; rather, consider whether some of your relationships are consistently draining and unhealthy.

I left my old social circle because it was a negative echo chamber. Instead of looking forward to a bright future, everyone was complaining about the things they didn't like about life.

Making new friends was difficult at first. The issue was that I couldn't provide any value to people with much more positive mindsets, the type of people I aspired to be like. That has changed, but it has taken time. Because of your new influences, once you find your "tribe," progress will come much more quickly.

Put your ideas to the test
It is not enough to try to ignore old thinking when it arises, as it will. We must question our assumptions. Is everything too expensive, or am I simply unable to afford it? Is it true that "people stink," or am I just looking for things to criticize? Compare your ideas to the evidence. If they fall apart under scrutiny, consider why you believed them in the first place. Your mindset will begin to evolve as you challenge your thoughts.

Positive media should be consumed
Consuming positive media on a daily basis will change your perspective by osmosis. "Positive media" is defined as anything that emphasizes the good in life or how to improve our own and others' living standards.

We've all heard that immersion is the best way to learn a new language. When you hear a new language on a daily basis, it begins to stick and becomes easier to remember. Soon, you'll not only understand but also speak that language.

New mindsets are the same; if you immerse yourself in personal growth content every day, you will change your mind's language. That language is your habitual self-dialogue, the way you speak to yourself at all times. Learn positive self-talk and you'll see the world in a new light.

Volunteer

Volunteering to help others can have a significant impact on how you feel about yourself and your perspective on the world. You can divert your attention away from your own problems by focusing on how you can help someone else. When you're looking for new ways to make someone else's situation better, it's easy to develop a positive mindset. You can't think about the bad while thinking about the good.

Avoid all negative news

Wars, murders, and politics all add to our mental baggage. However, it is understandable that the majority of the mainstream media focuses on bad news because tragedy sells. It makes no sense for us to sit around and stew over this bad news. It will almost certainly not allow for an optimal mindset, one that is focused on the best of what life has to offer.

By watching the news about a plane crash thousands of miles away, we are devoting our mental energy to something that will not benefit us. We can't change the bad things that are happening right now, but if we focus our attention on the things we can change, our lives will improve.

Make a plan of action

This is about considering the possibilities and then taking action to make them a reality. Thinking ahead will shift your focus from where you don't want to be to where you could be.

But simply writing it down isn't enough; we only grow when we take action. It's just a thought until we take action to make it a reality.

Don't know what steps to take? Don't worry, just figure out what the first thing you could do to get started, and then do it. Even if you make a mistake, you'll still make progress, which will keep you motivated to effect positive change. Never let analysis paralyze you. You have a vision; follow it.

Adopt a healthy way of life

A healthy body will aid in the maintenance of a healthy mind. Bad health was a major impediment during the most difficult period of my personal struggles. Chronic fatigue could knock me out for days.

Nonetheless, taking action, changing my diet, and working out laid the groundwork for all other changes to occur. My energy levels gradually increased to the point where my health was no longer an issue. Examine your sleeping habits, diet, and activity levels to see if there is anything that is sapping your energy. Sometimes laziness is simply exhaustion.

Thank you notes should be sent

Sending a thank you note can be an empowering gesture. A thank you note not only feels good, but it also fosters goodwill in others.

Because people like to feel appreciated, thank you notes will strengthen your relationships and connections. It makes no difference what they did; any small gesture you appreciated, from good service to a favor, qualifies you as a candidate. Send a quick email or a card in the mail to express your gratitude.

Establish a morning mindset routine

Making a mental list of everything we're looking forward to is a great way to start the day; it creates a sense of anticipation and excitement that creates momentum for the entire day.

Every morning, I listen to personal development videos or audiobooks. It is much easier to be happy and focused in the morning by focusing on the positive messages from this content. My work is completed more quickly, and it does not appear to be as difficult.

Make a success checklist

So you got off to a good start; now finish on a high note by making a mental list of the day's victories. It doesn't have to be spectacular; the goal of the exercise is simply to keep your focus on the best day of your life. Keep track of your losses; however, dwelling on them will kill your motivation and momentum. Finish strong, and waking up happy will be much easier.

Improving your life begins with a shift in your mindset. You, like me, may find that these steps are a good place to start.

Conclusion

In our lives, there are two kinds of moments. The first are those during which we feel positive emotions such as love, joy, equanimity, gratitude, or peace. The second type causes pits in our stomachs; these are times when we are suffering, feeling fear, anger, anxiety, malaise, or shame.

Negative emotions, on the other hand, have a place. Anger, for example, can serve as a motivator for purposeful action and personal growth on occasion. Fear can be beneficial in increasing our adrenaline during dangerous situations where we require enhanced senses and physical ability.

When mourning the loss of a friend or loved one, I believe sadness can be a rich and positive experience. As they say, it's better to have loved and lost someone than never to have loved at all.

Guilt is another one of those unpleasant emotions. It is triggered by the realization that we made a mistake that we would change if we could. Guilt, on the other hand, can be beneficial if it informs our future, motivating us to be better and more thoughtful in the future.

As a parent, I am constantly making mistakes that I am ashamed of. The key for me, however, is to learn from them rather than simply feeling like a bad father. That's when the real suffering begins.

When guilt becomes shame, it becomes destructive. Guilt is when you feel bad about an action you've taken, whereas shame is when you feel bad about yourself. It is critical to effectively manage guilt and keep it from turning into shame. **Here are some practical ways to stop feeling guilty:**

Positivity about oneself
This was mentioned previously, but it bears repeating for emphasis: The first mindset for dealing with guilt is admitting that what you're feeling guilty about is an action you've taken. It's perfectly normal and even healthy to feel guilty, as long as you don't associate it with

your own personality. This is the beginning of shame, and the path to the enormous guilt that many people feel for years after the original wrongdoing.

Always putting things right

I've read more parenting books than I can count, and trying to instill values in my children through discipline is one of my most difficult tasks as a parent. One excellent tip I've picked up is to always have the child "right the wrong." Make them write an apology note if they say something disrespectful. If they fail to turn in their homework, ensure that they complete it even if it is too late for them to receive credit in class. This will assist them in comprehending the process of removing guilt by addressing the action that resulted in negative feelings.

The first and most obvious step in implementing this is to define the action you'll take to right the wrong. It is critical that you emotionally connect that action with the moment you will be free of guilt. Simply put, figure out what is right, do it, acknowledge it, and move on.

Being Susceptible

We are most powerful when we are vulnerable. Putting ourselves out there has such a powerful effect. When we do this, our senses are stimulated, we speak from the heart, and the people in our lives pay attention to what we have to say. Admitting your mistake and apologizing can be therapeutic, even cathartic. It's a great way to put an end to guilt, even if the other party still holds grudges against you.

Do you know how crying makes you feel better? The same is true after you've allowed yourself to be vulnerable. Your words may not be perfect, and the other party may not be completely accepted, but the process of expressing yourself emotionally is deeply cleansing.

When you apologize or reconcile with someone you've wronged, you must give them your entire self. The only way to do this is to become uncomfortable and let it all hang out. Don't overthink or script your apology; simply tell them you have something to say and then start rolling. If what you're saying comes from your heart, the healing process will begin immediately.

Keeping Self-Compassion

We're harsh on ourselves. We criticize, judge, and label. Through our own critical self-talk, we transform guilt into shame. If we treated others the way we often treat ourselves, we'd be arrested.

To become more empathetic and compassionate with yourself, try the following technique: Put yourself in the shoes of a mother or father. A loving parent has more empathy and compassion than anyone else. You'll start telling yourself things like, "You're a good person, you're human, and you made a mistake, so just fix it and everything will be fine."

The ability to see a situation from a different angle is extremely powerful. It elicits a completely different set of emotions, and it serves as the foundation for the empathy required to be gentler on yourself and progress in growth.

Label It Modern psychology employs a technique known as "labeling." It's probably known by a variety of names, but the idea is to simply pay attention to your thoughts and emotions and recognize when you're feeling guilty. This technique has been used with great success in patients suffering from OCD, Tourette's Syndrome, depression, and a variety of other mental illnesses. It can certainly help you manage your guilt.

If you've never done this before, what I'm about to say may seem insane. But believe me when I say that if you practice and perfect it, you will understand its power. The simple act of recognizing and labeling the thought accomplishes an important task: it separates you from the thought. You no longer identify with the thought and instead recognize it for what it is: a feeling that exists in your mind but does not define you.

Try this simple technique the next time you feel guilty or any other negative emotion. Be present and tell yourself, "What I'm feeling is guilt," and just be with it and observe it for a few moments. Simply by separating guilt from your own sense of identity, you will have greatly reduced the likelihood of guilt becoming shame. If you want to take it a step further, tell yourself, "I don't need guilt now, so I'm going to let it go," and then imagine the thought floating away into space.

The average person spends approximately 100,000 minutes on Earth. Every day, we consume 70,000 of them, one-third of which is spent sleeping. Every moment we spend living with unnecessary guilt is a moment we will never get back. These are the kinds of moments that can never be enjoyed and in which no meaningful action can be taken. Manage your guilt and begin to reclaim the precious moments you have.

Made in the USA
Las Vegas, NV
16 December 2024

13767469R00022